Delicious
snacks

Delicious
snacks

Love Food ™ is an imprint of Parragon Books Ltd

Parragon
Queen Street House
4 Queen Street
Bath BA1 1HE

Cover and internal design by Mark Cavanagh
Introduction by Bridget Jones
Photography by Günter Beer
Additional photography by Clive Bozzard-Hill, Karen Thomas and Laurie Evans
Home Economists Stevan Paul, Sandra Baddeley, Sue Henderson, Valerie Berry, Annie
Rigg and Philippa Vanstone

ISBN 978-1-4054-9643-8
Printed in China

Notes for the reader
• This book uses metric and imperial measurement. Follow the same units of
measurement throughout, do not mix imperial and metric.
• All spoon measurements are level: teaspoons are assumed to be 5 ml, and
tablespoons are assumed to be 15 ml.
• Unless otherwise stated, milk is assumed to be low fat and eggs are medium. The
times given are an approximate guide only.
• Some recipes contain nuts. If you are allergic to nuts you should avoid using them
and any products containing nuts. Recipes using raw or very lightly cooked eggs
should be avoided by infants, the elderly, pregnant women, convalescents and anyone
suffering from illness.

Contents

Snacks

Juggling duty and desire is part of the modern lifestyle, and the way we eat matches our kaleidoscope of commitments. Many people work away from home and each day is not necessarily identical to the last. There are frequent days when family members are busy with separate activities and need to eat at different times. It is therefore not always easy to plan for, prepare and eat formal meals. Eating small amounts frequently fits busy lifestyles – snatched breakfasts, mid-morning snacks, packed lunches, after-work snacks and late, but light, suppers are typical eating occasions.

Social snacking

From a casual buffet to a formal canapé party, festive gatherings are classic snacking occasions. When feeding a crowd, two or three home-made items will transform a basic selection of nuts, crisps, crackers and other bought snacks, making them more interesting and substantial.

Here are some tips to make entertaining easy:
• The best party snacks can be prepared ahead and cooked at the last minute with minimum fuss, or served cold.
• Fit the presentation to the occasion – snacks lined up on platters with stylish garnishes look impressive.
• Instead of plates, have bright paper napkins to wipe sticky fingers.
• Put out bowls where guests can deposit discarded cocktail sticks.
• Stagger snacks during a party, handing out alternating trays of different types.

Minimum effort: maximum flavour

Take-away food tends to be full of fat, misses out on good nutrients, and comes in portion sizes that make us eat more than we need. The TV Snacks chapter has recipes that are the right compromise for times

when slaving over a hot hob is not an option. Unlike their bought counterparts, these are free from artificial additives, and are fresh and delicious. Oven-fried Chicken Wings, Home-made Oven Fries, and Classic Spare Ribs need minimum attention once they're in the oven. Add a bag of prepared salad and follow on with some fresh fruit for a vitamin boost.

Light lunches or late nights

Lighter eating is good when working late, socialising early evening, or providing a cab service for children's out-of-school activities. It's often late evening before there's a chance to sit and eat, and satisfying but light dishes are best. Eating light occasionally is also good for keeping weight in check. Spicy Prawns, Parma Ham with Melon & Asparagus, or Red Cabbage Slaw are good examples of suitable dishes. Keep breads in the freezer, ready cut for thawing in the microwave – ciabatta, bagels, crusty French or close-textured light rye make

light dishes more substantial. Instant couscous can be ready in minutes to complement light dishes without making them too stodgy.

Eating out and about

Here are a few reminders for practical packed lunches:
• Use insulated containers and/or bags and drinks holders to keep food fresh. They come in all sizes, from individual pots to picnic hampers for a feast.
• For warming drinks or soups, small Thermos flasks are ideal. Insulated pots are good for chunky soups or stews.
• Fresh fruit and/or salad or raw vegetable sticks are vital in daily packed lunches. For salads on the go, make sure to pack dressings in a screw-top pot and add them at the last minute to keep salad leaves crisp.
• Try cook-ahead foods for a meal one day and packed lunch the next: make Spanish Omelette for supper, and chill some for a packed lunch. Soups and sushi can also be prepared ahead.

1

Mouth-watering Morsels

serves 4

3 skinless, boneless chicken breasts

4 tbsp wholemeal plain flour

1 tbsp wheatgerm

1/2 tsp ground cumin

1/2 tsp ground coriander

pepper

1 egg, lightly beaten

2 tbsp olive oil

green salad, to serve

for the dipping sauce

100 g/3½ oz sunblush tomatoes

100 g/3½ oz fresh tomatoes, peeled, deseeded and chopped

2 tbsp mayonnaise

chicken nuggets

Preheat the oven to 190°C/375°F/Gas Mark 5. Cut the chicken breasts into 4-cm/1½-inch chunks. Mix the flour, wheatgerm, cumin, coriander, and pepper to taste in a bowl, then divide in half and put on 2 separate plates. Put the beaten egg on a third plate.

Pour the oil into a baking tray and heat in the oven. Roll the chicken pieces in one plate of flour, shake to remove any excess, then roll in the egg and in the second plate of flour, again shaking off any excess flour. When all the nuggets are ready, remove the baking tray from the oven and toss the nuggets in the hot oil. Roast in the oven for 25–30 minutes until golden and crisp.

Meanwhile, to make the dipping sauce, put both kinds of tomatoes in a blender or food processor and process until smooth. Add the mayonnaise and process again until well combined.

Remove the nuggets from the oven and drain on kitchen paper. Serve with the dipping sauce and a green salad.

serves 4

115 g/4 oz sirloin or rump
steak

4 button mushrooms,
cut into 1-cm/$1/2$-inch cubes

$1/2$ small onion, cut into
1-cm/$1/2$-inch cubes

for the spicy tomato
marinade

50 ml/2 fl oz tomato juice

50 ml/2 fl oz beef stock

1 tbsp Worcestershire sauce

1 tbsp lemon juice

2 tbsp dry sherry

few drops of Tabasco sauce

2 tbsp vegetable oil

1 tbsp minced celery

miniature beef kebabs

Cut the steak into 1-cm/$1/2$-inch cubes. Combine all the marinade ingredients in a large, non-metallic bowl, whisk well and stir in the meat, mushrooms and onion. Cover the bowl with clingfilm and place in the refrigerator to marinate for 30 minutes.

Drain off the marinade. Place alternating pieces of steak and vegetables on cocktail sticks, taking care not to pack them together too tightly.

Preheat a griddle or heavy-based frying pan over a high heat. Place the kebabs in the pan and cook, turning frequently, for 5 minutes, or until gently browned and cooked through.

Pile the kebabs high on platters and serve immediately.

serves 4

450 g/1 lb lean, finely
minced lamb

1 medium onion

1 garlic clove, crushed

25 g/1 oz fresh white or
brown breadcrumbs

1 tbsp chopped fresh mint

1 tbsp chopped fresh parsley

salt and pepper

1 egg, beaten

olive oil, for brushing

warm pitta bread and salad,
to serve

grecian meatballs

Put the minced lamb in a bowl. Grate in the onion, then add the garlic, breadcrumbs, mint and parsley. Season well with salt and pepper. Mix the ingredients well then add the beaten egg and mix to bind the mixture together. Alternatively, the ingredients can be mixed in a food processor.

With damp hands, form the mixture into 16 small balls and thread onto 4 flat metal skewers. Lightly oil a grill pan and brush the meatballs with oil.

Preheat the grill and cook the meatballs under a medium heat for 10 minutes, turning frequently, and brushing with more oil if necessary, until browned. Serve the meatballs tucked into warm pitta bread with salad.

serves 2

6 tbsp mayonnaise

2 garlic cloves, crushed

2 large white fish
fillets, skinned

1 egg, beaten

3 heaped tbsp plain flour

vegetable oil, for deep-frying

lemon wedges, to garnish

fish goujons with garlic mayonnaise

Combine the mayonnaise and garlic in a small dish. Cover with clingfilm and refrigerate while you cook the fish.

Cut the fish into 2.5-cm/1-inch strips. Dip the strips in the egg, then drain and dredge in flour.

Meanwhile, heat the oil in a deep-fryer or large saucepan to 180–190°C/350–375°F, or until a cube of bread browns in 30 seconds. Fry the pieces of fish in the hot oil for 3–4 minutes, or until golden brown. Remove from the oil and drain on a dish lined with kitchen paper.

Remove the garlic mayonnaise from the refrigerator and stir once. Serve the fish on an attractive dish, garnished with lemon wedges, with the mayonnaise on the side for dipping.

makes 20

200 g/7 oz canned tuna in
spring water, drained

1 egg, beaten

1 tsp finely chopped
fresh parsley

sea salt and pepper

50 g/1³/4 oz fresh wholemeal
breadcrumbs

about 1 tbsp wholemeal
plain flour

vegetable oil, for brushing

tuna bites

Mash the tuna with the egg, parsley, a pinch of salt and pepper
to taste. Add the breadcrumbs and mix well, then add enough of
the flour to bind the mixture together.

Divide the mixture into 20 mini portions, shape each portion
into a ball and chill for 15 minutes.

Meanwhile, preheat the oven to 190°C/375°F/Gas Mark 5. Brush a
non-stick baking sheet with a little oil. Space the tuna balls out
on the baking sheet and brush with a little more oil. Bake in the
preheated oven for 15–20 minutes until golden and crisp.

Remove from the oven and drain on kitchen paper. Serve warm
or cold.

serves 4

225 g/8 oz dried chickpeas

1 large onion, finely chopped

1 garlic clove, crushed

2 tbsp chopped fresh parsley,
plus extra sprigs to garnish

2 tsp ground cumin

2 tsp ground coriander

1/2 tsp baking powder

cayenne pepper

salt

oil, for deep-frying

to serve

hummus (see page 84)

tomato wedges

pitta bread

falafel

Soak the chickpeas overnight in enough cold water to cover them and allow room for expansion. Drain, then place in a saucepan, cover with fresh water and bring to the boil. Reduce the heat and simmer for 1 hour, or until tender. Drain.

Place the chickpeas in a food processor and blend to make a coarse paste. Add the onion, garlic, parsley, cumin, coriander, baking powder, and cayenne pepper and salt to taste. Blend again to mix thoroughly.

Cover and leave to rest for 30 minutes, then shape into 8 balls. Leave to rest for a further 30 minutes. Heat the oil in a wok or large saucepan to 180–190°C/350–375°F, or until a cube of bread browns in 30 seconds. Gently drop in the balls and cook until golden brown. Remove from the oil and drain on a plate lined with kitchen paper.

Serve hot or at room temperature with hummus, tomato wedges and pitta bread. Garnish with sprigs of parsley.

serves 4

115 g/4 oz fresh white bread

2 tbsp freshly grated
Parmesan cheese

1 tsp paprika

2 egg whites

225 g/8 oz button
mushrooms

for the aïoli

4 garlic cloves, crushed

salt and pepper

2 egg yolks

225 ml/8 fl oz extra-virgin
olive oil

mushroom bites with aïoli

Preheat the oven to 190°C/375°F/Gas Mark 5. To make the aïoli, put the garlic in a bowl, add a pinch of salt and mash with the back of a spoon. Add the egg yolks and beat with an electric whisk for 30 seconds, or until creamy. Start beating in the oil, one drop at a time. As the mixture begins to thicken, add the oil in a steady stream, beating constantly. Season to taste with salt and pepper, cover the bowl with clingfilm and chill in the refrigerator until required.

Line a large baking sheet with baking paper. Grate the bread into breadcrumbs and place them in a bowl with the Parmesan cheese and paprika. Lightly whisk the egg whites in a separate clean bowl, then dip each mushroom first into the egg whites, then into the breadcrumbs, and place on the prepared baking sheet.

Bake in the preheated oven for 15 minutes, or until the coating is crisp and golden. Serve immediately with the aïoli.

serves 8

4 garlic cloves, peeled

2 tsp coriander seeds

1 small lemon

450 g/1 lb canned or bottled
large green stoned olives,
drained

4 fresh thyme sprigs

4 feathery stalks of fennel

2 small fresh red chillies
(optional)

pepper

extra-virgin olive oil

spicy marinated olives

Using the flat side of a broad knife, lightly crush each garlic clove. Using a pestle and mortar, crack the coriander seeds. Cut the lemon, with its rind, into small chunks.

Place the olives, garlic, coriander seeds, lemon chunks, thyme sprigs, fennel and chillies, if using, in a large bowl and toss together. Season to taste with pepper, but you should not need to add salt as canned or bottled olives are usually salty enough. Pack the ingredients tightly into a glass jar with a lid. Pour in enough olive oil to cover the olives, then seal the jar tightly.

Leave the olives at room temperature for 24 hours, then marinate in the refrigerator for at least 1 week but preferably 2 weeks before serving. From time to time, gently give the jar a shake to re-mix the ingredients. Return the olives to room temperature and remove from the oil to serve. Provide wooden cocktail sticks for spearing the olives.

serves 4

sunflower oil, for
deep-frying

1 large egg

pinch of salt

175 ml/6 fl oz water

55 g/2 oz plain flour

2 tsp ground cinnamon

55 g/2 oz caster sugar

4 eating apples, peeled
and cored

apple fritters

Pour the sunflower oil into a deep fryer or large, heavy-based saucepan and heat to 180–190°C/350–375°F, or until a cube of bread browns in 30 seconds.

Meanwhile, using an electric mixer, beat the egg and salt together until frothy, then quickly whisk in the water and flour. Do not overbeat the batter – it doesn't matter if it isn't completely smooth.

Mix the cinnamon and sugar together in a shallow dish and reserve.

Slice the apples into 5-mm/$1/4$-inch thick rings. Spear with a fork, 1 slice at a time, and dip in the batter to coat. Add to the hot oil, in batches, and cook for 1 minute on each side, or until golden and puffed up. Remove with a slotted spoon and drain on kitchen paper. Keep warm while you cook the remaining batches. Transfer to a large serving plate, sprinkle with the cinnamon sugar and serve.

serves 6

600 ml/1 pint good-quality
ice cream

200 g/7 oz plain chocolate

2 tbsp unsalted butter

chocolate ice-cream bites

Line a baking tray with clingfilm.

Using a melon baller, scoop out balls of ice cream and place them on the prepared baking tray. Alternatively, cut the ice cream into bite-size cubes. Stick a cocktail stick in each piece and return to the freezer until very hard.

Place the chocolate and the butter in a heatproof bowl set over a saucepan of gently simmering water until melted. Quickly dip the frozen ice-cream balls into the warm chocolate and return to the freezer. Keep them there until ready to serve.

TV Snacks

makes 8

4 muffins

125 ml/4 fl oz ready-made
tomato pizza sauce

2 sun-dried tomatoes
in oil, chopped

55 g/2 oz Parma ham

2 rings canned
pineapple, chopped

1/2 green pepper, deseeded
and chopped

125 g/4 1/2 oz mozzarella
cheese, cubed

olive oil, for drizzling

salt and pepper

fresh basil leaves, to garnish

ham & pineapple muffin pizzas

Preheat the grill to medium. Cut the muffins in half and toast the cut side lightly.

Spread the tomato sauce evenly over the muffins. Sprinkle the sun-dried tomatoes on top of the tomato sauce. Cut the Parma ham into thin strips and place on the muffins with the pineapple and pepper. Carefully arrange the mozzarella cubes on top.

Drizzle a little oil over each pizza and add salt and pepper to taste.

Place under the hot grill and cook until the cheese melts and bubbles. Serve immediately, garnished with basil leaves.

serves 4

900 g/2 lb pork spare ribs

2 tbsp dark soy sauce

3 tbsp hoisin sauce

1 tbsp Chinese rice wine or dry sherry

pinch of Chinese five spice powder

2 tsp dark brown sugar

1/4 tsp chilli sauce

2 garlic cloves, crushed

coriander sprigs, to garnish

classic spare ribs

Cut the spare ribs into separate pieces if they are joined together. If desired, you can chop them into 5-cm/2-inch lengths, using a cleaver.

Mix together the soy sauce, hoisin sauce, Chinese rice wine or sherry, Chinese five spice powder, dark brown sugar, chilli sauce and garlic in a large bowl.

Place the ribs in a shallow dish and pour the mixture over them, turning to coat them well. Cover and marinate in the refrigerator, turning the ribs from time to time, for at least 1 hour.

Remove the ribs from the marinade and arrange them in a single layer on a wire rack placed over a roasting tin half-filled with warm water. Brush with the marinade, reserving the remainder.

Cook in a preheated oven, at 180°C/350°F/Gas Mark 4, for 30 minutes. Remove the roasting tin from the oven and turn the ribs over. Brush with the remaining marinade and return to the oven for a further 30 minutes, or until cooked through. Transfer to a warmed serving dish, garnish with the coriander sprigs and serve immediately.

serves 4

2 tbsp vegetable or
groundnut oil

1 tbsp sesame oil

juice of 1/2 lime

2 skinless, boneless chicken
breasts, cut into small cubes

for the dip

2 tbsp vegetable or
groundnut oil

1 small onion, chopped finely

1 small fresh green chilli,
deseeded and chopped

1 garlic clove, chopped finely

125 ml/4 fl oz crunchy
peanut butter

6–8 tbsp water

juice of 1/2 lime

crushed peanuts, to garnish

chicken satay

Combine both the oils and the lime juice in a non-metallic dish. Add the chicken cubes, cover with clingfilm and chill for 1 hour.

To make the dip, heat the oil in a frying pan and fry the onion, chilli and garlic over a low heat, stirring occasionally, for about 5 minutes, until just softened. Add the peanut butter, water and lime juice and simmer gently, stirring constantly, until the peanut butter has softened enough to make a dip – you may need to add extra water to make a thinner consistency.

Meanwhile, drain the chicken cubes and thread them onto 8–12 presoaked wooden skewers. Put under a hot grill or on a barbecue, turning frequently, for about 10 minutes, until cooked and browned. Serve hot with the warm dip, garnished with crushed peanuts.

serves 4

12 chicken wings

1 egg

50 ml/2 fl oz milk

4 heaped tbsp plain flour

1 tsp paprika

salt and pepper

225 g/8 oz breadcrumbs

55 g/2 oz butter

oven-fried chicken wings

Preheat the oven to 220°C/425°F/Gas Mark 7. Separate the chicken wings into 3 pieces each. Discard the bony tip. Beat the egg with the milk in a shallow dish. Combine the flour, paprika and salt and pepper to taste in a separate shallow dish. Place the breadcrumbs in another shallow dish.

Dip the chicken pieces into the egg to coat well, then drain and roll in the seasoned flour. Remove, shaking off any excess, and roll the chicken in the breadcrumbs, gently pressing them onto the surface, then shaking off any excess.

Melt the butter in the preheated oven in a shallow roasting tin large enough to hold all the chicken pieces in a single layer. Arrange the chicken, skin-side down, in the tin and bake in the oven for 10 minutes. Turn and bake for a further 10 minutes, or until the chicken is tender and the juices run clear when a skewer is inserted into the thickest part of the meat.

Remove the chicken from the tin and arrange on a large platter. Serve hot or at room temperature.

serves 6

400 g/14 oz canned
white crabmeat

1–2 fresh bird's eye
chillies, to taste, deseeded
and finely chopped

6 spring onions,
finely shredded

1 courgette, grated

1 carrot, grated

1 small yellow pepper,
deseeded and finely
shredded

85 g/3 oz fresh beansprouts,
rinsed

1 tbsp chopped fresh
coriander

1 large egg white

1–2 tbsp sunflower oil

for the salsa

1 bird's eye chilli, deseeded
and finely chopped

5-cm/2-inch piece
cucumber, grated

1 tbsp chopped fresh
coriander

1 tbsp lime juice

1 tbsp Thai sweet chilli sauce

1 tbsp peanuts, finely
chopped (optional)

thai-style fish cakes

Mix all the fish cake ingredients, except for the egg white and oil, together. Whisk the egg white until frothy and just beginning to stiffen then stir into the crab mixture. Then, using your hands, press about 1–2 tablespoons of the mixture together to form a fish cake. Repeat until 12 fish cakes are formed.

Make the salsa by combining all the ingredients except for the peanuts. Spoon into a small bowl, cover and leave for 30 minutes for the flavours to develop. Sprinkle with the peanuts, if using.

Heat 1 teaspoon of the oil in a non-stick frying pan over a low heat. Cook the fish cakes in batches for 2 minutes on each side over a medium heat until lightly browned. Take care when turning them over. Remove and drain on kitchen paper. Repeat until all the fish cakes are cooked, using more oil if necessary. Serve immediately with the salsa.

serves 6

175 g/6 oz tortilla chips

400 g/14 oz canned refried beans, warmed

2 tbsp finely chopped bottled jalapeño chillies

200 g/7 oz canned or bottled pimentos or roasted peppers, drained and finely sliced

salt and pepper

115 g/4 oz Gruyère cheese, grated

115 g/4 oz Cheddar cheese, grated

nachos

Preheat the oven to 200°C/400°F/Gas Mark 6.

Spread the tortilla chips out over the base of a large, shallow, ovenproof dish or roasting tin. Cover with the warmed refried beans. Scatter over the chillies and pimentos and season to taste with salt and pepper. Mix the cheeses together in a bowl and sprinkle on top.

Bake in the preheated oven for 5–8 minutes, or until the cheese is bubbling and melted. Serve immediately.

serves 4
150 g/5¹/₂ oz long-grain rice
3 eggs, beaten
2 tbsp vegetable oil
2 garlic cloves, crushed
4 spring onions, chopped
125 g/4¹/₂ oz cooked peas
1 tbsp light soy sauce
pinch of salt
shredded spring onion,
to garnish

egg fried rice

Cook the rice in a pan of boiling water for 10–12 minutes, until almost cooked, but not soft. Drain well, rinse under cold water and drain again.

Place the beaten eggs in a non-stick saucepan and cook over a gentle heat, stirring until softly scrambled.

Heat the vegetable oil in a preheated wok or large frying pan, swirling the oil around the base of the wok until it is really hot.

Add the crushed garlic, spring onions and peas and sauté, stirring occasionally, for 1–2 minutes. Stir the rice into the wok, mixing to combine.

Add the eggs, light soy sauce and a pinch of salt to the wok or frying pan and stir to mix the egg in thoroughly.

Transfer the egg fried rice to serving dishes and serve garnished with the shredded spring onion.

serves 4

4 x 225 g/8 oz baking potatoes

2 tsp olive oil

coarse sea salt and pepper

for the guacamole dip

175 g/6 oz ripe avocado

1 tbsp lemon juice

2 ripe, firm tomatoes, chopped finely

1 tsp grated lemon rind

100 g/3^1/$_2$ oz low-fat soft cheese with herbs and garlic

4 spring onions, chopped finely

a few drops of Tabasco sauce

salt and pepper, to taste

potato skins with guacamole

Bake the potatoes in a preheated oven at 200°C/400°F/Gas Mark 6 for 1^1/$_4$ hours. Remove from the oven and allow to cool for 30 minutes. Reset the oven to 220°C/425°F/Gas Mark 7.

Halve the potatoes lengthwise and scoop out 2 tablespoons of the flesh. Place the skins on a baking tray sheet and brush the flesh side lightly with oil. Sprinkle with salt and pepper. Bake for a further 25 minutes until golden and crisp.

To make the guacamole dip, mash the avocado with the lemon juice. Add the remaining ingredients and mix. Transfer to a serving bowl.

Drain the potato skins on paper towels and transfer to a warmed serving platter. Serve hot with the guacamole dip.

serves 4

450 g/1 lb potatoes, peeled

2 tbsp sunflower oil

salt and pepper

ketchup and mayonnaise,
to serve (optional)

home-made oven fries

Preheat the oven to 200°C/400°F/Gas Mark 6.

Cut the potatoes into thick, even-sized chips. Rinse them under cold running water, then dry well on a clean tea towel. Put in a bowl, add the oil and toss together until thoroughly coated.

Spread the chips on a baking sheet and cook in the preheated oven for 40–45 minutes, turning once, until golden. Add salt and pepper to taste and serve hot with ketchup and mayonnaise, if desired.

makes about 250 g/9 oz

3 tbsp sunflower oil

70 g/2$^{1}/_{2}$ oz popcorn

25 g/1 oz butter

55 g/2 oz light soft brown sugar

2 tbsp golden syrup

1 tbsp milk

55 g/2 oz plain chocolate chips

chocolate popcorn

Preheat the oven to 150°C/300°F/Gas Mark 2. Heat the oil in a large, heavy-based saucepan. Add the popcorn, cover the saucepan, and cook, shaking the saucepan vigorously and frequently, for about 2 minutes, until the popping stops. Turn into a large bowl.

Put the butter, sugar, golden syrup and milk in a saucepan and heat gently until the butter has melted. Bring to the boil, without stirring, and boil for 2 minutes. Remove from the heat, add the chocolate chips, and stir until melted.

Pour the chocolate mixture over the popcorn and toss together until evenly coated. Spread the mixture onto a large baking tray.

Bake the popcorn in the oven for about 15 minutes, until crisp. Leave to cool before serving.

3

Lighter Bites

serves 4

4 fillet steaks, about 115 g/
4 oz each, fat discarded

2 tbsp red wine vinegar

2 tbsp orange juice

2 tsp ready-made English
mustard

2 eggs

175 g/6 oz baby new potatoes

115 g/4 oz French beans,
trimmed

175 g/6 oz mixed salad
leaves, such as baby spinach,
rocket and mizuna

1 yellow pepper, peeled,
skinned and cut into strips

175 g/6 oz cherry tomatoes,
halved

black olives, stoned (optional)

2 tsp extra-virgin olive oil

pepper

warm beef niçoise

Place the steaks in a shallow dish. Blend the vinegar with
1 tablespoon of the orange juice and 1 teaspoon of the mustard.
Pour over the steaks, cover and leave in the refrigerator for at least
30 minutes. Turn over halfway through the marinating time.

Place the eggs in a pan and cover with cold water. Bring to the
boil, then reduce the heat to a simmer and cook for 10 minutes.
Remove and plunge the eggs into cold water. Once cold, shell
and reserve.

Meanwhile, place the potatoes in a saucepan and cover with
cold water. Bring to the boil, cover and simmer for 15 minutes, or
until tender when pierced with a fork. Drain and reserve.

Bring a saucepan of water to the boil. Add the beans, cover and
simmer for 5–8 minutes, or until tender. Drain, plunge into cold
water then drain again and reserve. Meanwhile, arrange the
potatoes and beans on top of the salad leaves together with the
yellow pepper, cherry tomatoes and olives, if using. Chop the
hard-boiled eggs into wedges and add to the salad. Blend the
remaining orange juice and mustard with the olive oil, season to
taste with pepper and reserve.

Heat a griddle pan until smoking. Drain the steaks and cook for
3–5 minutes on each side or according to personal preference.
Slice the steaks and arrange on top of the salad, then pour over
the dressing and serve.

serves 4

225 g/8 oz baby asparagus spears

1 small or 1/2 medium-sized Galia or Canteloupe melon

55 g/2 oz Parma ham, thinly sliced

150 g/51/2 oz bag of mixed salad leaves, such as herb salad with rocket

85 g/3 oz fresh raspberries

1 tbsp freshly shaved Parmesan cheese

1 tbsp balsamic vinegar

2 tbsp raspberry vinegar

2 tbsp orange juice

parma ham with melon & asparagus

Trim the asparagus, cutting in half if very long. Cook in lightly boiled water over a medium heat for 5 minutes, or until tender. Drain and plunge into cold water then drain again and reserve.

Cut the melon in half and scoop out the seeds. Cut into small wedges and cut away the rind. Separate the Parma ham, cut the slices in half and wrap around the melon wedges.

Arrange the salad leaves on a large serving platter and place the melon wedges on top together with the asparagus spears.

Scatter over the raspberries and Parmesan shavings. Place the vinegars and orange juice in a screw-top jar and shake until blended. Pour over the salad and serve.

serves 4

4 skinless, boneless chicken
breasts, about 140 g/5 oz each

4 tsp Cajun seasoning

2 tsp sunflower oil

1 ripe mango, peeled, stoned
and cut into thick slices

200 g/7 oz mixed salad leaves

1 red onion, thinly sliced
and cut in half

175 g/6 oz cooked beetroot,
diced

85 g/3 oz radishes, sliced

55 g/2 oz walnut halves

4 tbsp walnut oil

1–2 tsp Dijon mustard

1 tbsp lemon juice

salt and pepper

2 tbsp sesame seeds

cajun chicken salad

Make 3 diagonal slashes across each chicken breast. Put the
chicken into a shallow dish and sprinkle all over with the Cajun
seasoning. Cover and refrigerate for at least 30 minutes.

When ready to cook, brush a griddle pan with the sunflower oil.
Heat over a high heat until very hot and a few drops of water
sprinkled into the pan sizzle immediately. Add the chicken and
cook for 7–8 minutes on each side, or until thoroughly cooked. If
still slightly pink in the centre, cook a little longer. Remove the
chicken and reserve.

Add the mango slices to the pan and cook for 2 minutes on each
side. Remove and reserve.

Meanwhile, arrange the salad leaves in a salad bowl and scatter
over the onion, beetroot, radishes and walnut halves.

Put the walnut oil, mustard, lemon juice, and salt and pepper to
taste in a screw-top jar and shake until well blended. Pour over
the salad and sprinkle with the sesame seeds.

Add the mango and chicken to the salad bowl and serve
immediately.

serves 4

115 g/4 oz cherry or baby
plum tomatoes

several lettuce leaves

4 ripe tomatoes, roughly
chopped

100 g/3½ oz smoked salmon

200 g/7 oz large cooked
prawns, thawed if frozen

1 tbsp Dijon mustard

2 tsp caster sugar

2 tsp red wine vinegar

2 tbsp medium olive oil

few fresh dill sprigs

pepper

warmed rolls or ciabatta
bread, to serve

tomato, salmon & prawn salad

Halve most of the cherry tomatoes. Place the lettuce leaves around the edge of a shallow bowl and add all the tomatoes and cherry tomatoes. Using scissors, snip the smoked salmon into strips and scatter over the tomatoes, then add the prawns.

Mix the mustard, sugar, vinegar and oil together in a small bowl, then tear most of the dill sprigs into it. Mix well and pour over the salad. Toss well to coat the salad with the dressing. Snip the remaining dill over the top and season to taste with pepper.

Serve the salad with warmed rolls or ciabatta bread.

serves 4

24 raw tiger prawns, thawed if frozen

1 bay leaf

2 tbsp lime juice

1 tsp hot paprika

salt and pepper

2 shallots, coarsely chopped

1 garlic clove, coarsely chopped

1 tbsp light soy sauce

1 tbsp peanuts

1 tbsp desiccated coconut

1/2 red pepper, deseeded and chopped

200 g/7 oz canned tomatoes

sunflower oil, for brushing

lime wedges, to garnish

spicy prawns

Pull the heads off the prawns and peel off the shells. Place the heads, shells and bay leaf in a saucepan and add enough cold water to cover. Bring to the boil, then lower the heat and simmer for 30 minutes.

Meanwhile, using a sharp knife, cut along the back of each prawn. Remove the dark vein with the point of the knife. Place the prawns in a non-metallic dish and sprinkle with the lime juice and paprika. Season with salt and pepper and toss well to coat. Cover with clingfilm and leave to marinate in the refrigerator.

Put the shallots, garlic, soy sauce, peanuts, coconut and red pepper in a food processor. Drain the tomatoes, reserving 5 tablespoons of the can juice. Add the tomatoes and the reserved can juice to the food processor. Process until smooth. Scrape the mixture into a saucepan.

When the shellfish stock is ready, strain it into a measuring jug, pour it into the saucepan and bring the mixture to the boil, stirring occasionally. Lower the heat and simmer for 25–30 minutes until thickened.

Brush a griddle with oil and preheat. Remove the prawns from the refrigerator and thread them loosely onto skewers to make handling them easier. When the griddle is hot, add the prawns and cook for 2 minutes, or until they have changed colour and are cooked through.

Transfer the prawns to a serving dish – with or without the skewers – and garnish with lime wedges. Pour the dipping sauce into a bowl and serve with the prawns.

serves 4

olive oil, for brushing and
drizzling

1 red pepper, halved and
deseeded

1 orange pepper, halved and
deseeded

4 thick slices baguette or
ciabatta

1 fennel bulb, sliced

1 red onion, sliced

2 courgettes, sliced
diagonally

2 garlic cloves, halved

1 tomato, halved

salt and pepper

fresh sage leaves, to garnish

mixed vegetable bruschetta

Brush a griddle with oil and preheat. Cut each pepper half lengthways into 4 strips. Toast the bread slices on both sides in a toaster or under the grill.

When the griddle is hot add the peppers and fennel and cook for 4 minutes, then add the onion and courgettes and cook for a further 5 minutes until all the vegetables are tender but still with a slight 'bite'. If necessary, cook the vegetables in 2 batches, as they should be placed on the griddle in a single layer.

Meanwhile, rub the garlic halves over the toasts, then rub them with the tomato halves. Place on warm plates. Pile the grilled vegetables on top of the toasts, drizzle with olive oil and season with salt and pepper. Garnish with sage leaves and serve warm.

serves 4

280 g/10 oz mozzarella
di bufala, drained and
sliced thinly

8 plum tomatoes, sliced

salt and pepper

20 fresh basil leaves

125 ml/4 fl oz extra-virgin
olive oil

three-colour salad

Arrange the cheese and tomato slices on 4 individual serving plates and season to taste with salt. Set aside in a cool place for 30 minutes.

Sprinkle the basil leaves over the salad and drizzle with the olive oil. Season with pepper and serve immediately.

serves 6

450 g/1 lb red cabbage

1 eating apple

4 tbsp orange juice

1 large carrot, peeled and grated

1 red onion, peeled and cut into tiny wedges

175 g/6 oz cherry tomatoes, halved

7.5-cm/3-inch piece cucumber, peeled if preferred, and diced

55 g/2 oz fresh dates, stoned and chopped

1 tbsp extra-virgin olive oil

1 tbsp chopped fresh flat-leaf parsley

pepper

red cabbage slaw

Discard the outer leaves and hard central core from the cabbage and shred finely. Wash thoroughly in plenty of cold water then shake dry and place in a salad bowl.

Core the apple and chop, toss in 1 tablespoon of the orange juice, then add to the salad bowl together with the carrot, onion, tomatoes, cucumber and dates.

Place the remaining orange juice in a screw-top jar, add the oil, parsley and pepper and shake until blended. Pour the dressing over the salad, toss lightly and serve.

serves 4–6

225–300 g/8–10^1/$_2$ oz mixed
soft fruits, such as blueberries,
raspberries and stoned fresh
cherries

1^1/$_2$–2 tbsp Cointreau or
orange flower water

250 g/9 oz mascarpone
cheese

200 ml/7 fl oz crème fraîche

2–3 tbsp dark muscovado
sugar

cheat's crème brûlée

Prepare the fruit, if necessary, and lightly rinse, then place in the bases of 4–6 x 150 ml/5 fl oz ramekin dishes. Sprinkle the fruit with the Cointreau or orange flower water.

Cream the mascarpone cheese in a bowl until soft, then gradually beat in the crème fraîche.

Spoon the cheese mixture over the fruit, smoothing the surface and ensuring that the tops are level. Chill in the refrigerator for at least 2 hours.

Sprinkle the tops with the sugar. Using a chef's blow torch, grill the tops until caramelized (about 2–3 minutes). Alternatively, cook under a preheated grill, turning the dishes, for 3–4 minutes, or until the tops are lightly caramelized all over.

Serve immediately or chill in the refrigerator for 15–20 minutes before serving.

makes 4

a selection of fruit,
such as apricots, peaches,
figs, strawberries, mangoes,
pineapple, bananas, dates
and pawpaw, prepared and
cut into chunks

maple syrup

50 g/1³/4 oz plain chocolate
(minimum 70% cocoa solids),
broken into chunks

fruit skewers

Soak 4 bamboo skewers in water for at least 20 minutes.

Preheat the grill to high and line the grill pan with foil. Thread alternate pieces of fruit onto each skewer. Brush the fruit with a little maple syrup.

Put the chocolate in a heatproof bowl, set the bowl over a saucepan of barely simmering water and heat until it is melted.

Meanwhile, cook the skewers under the preheated grill for 3 minutes, or until caramelized. Serve drizzled with a little of the melted chocolate.

Food on the Go

serves 4

15 g/1/2 oz butter

1/2 red onion, finely chopped

1 leek, chopped

1 garlic clove, crushed

1 carrot, peeled and grated

1 potato, peeled and grated

300 ml/10 fl oz vegetable stock

500 g/1 lb 2 oz ripe tomatoes, peeled, deseeded and chopped

1 tbsp tomato purée

sea salt and pepper

150 ml/5 fl oz full-fat milk

snipped chives, to garnish (optional)

slices of seeded bread, to serve

creamy tomato soup

Melt the butter in a large saucepan over a low heat and cook the onion, leek and garlic for 10 minutes, or until very soft but not browned.

Add the carrot and potato and cook for 5 minutes. Add the stock and bring up to simmering point.

Add the tomatoes and tomato purée and season to taste with salt and pepper. Simmer for 15 minutes until the vegetables are very soft. Add the milk and warm through, then transfer the soup to a blender or food processor and process until very smooth. You can pass the soup through a sieve at this stage, if you like.

Return the soup to the rinsed-out saucepan and reheat gently. Garnish the soup with snipped chives, if desired, and serve with slices of seeded bread.

serves 4–6

400g/14 oz can refried beans

8 flour tortillas

200 g/7 oz Cheddar cheese, grated

1 onion, chopped

1/2 bunch fresh coriander leaves, chopped, plus extra leaves to garnish

for the tomato salsa

6–8 ripe tomatoes, finely chopped

about 100 ml/3$\frac{1}{2}$ fl oz tomato juice

3–4 garlic cloves, finely chopped

1/2 bunch fresh coriander leaves, coarsely chopped

pinch of sugar

3–4 fresh green chillies, deseeded and finely chopped

1/2–1 tsp ground cumin

3–4 spring onions, finely chopped

salt

cheese & bean quesadillas

To make the tomato salsa, stir all the ingredients together in a bowl and season with salt to taste. Cover with clingfilm and chill in the refrigerator until required.

Place the beans in a small pan and set over a low heat to warm through.

Meanwhile, make the tortillas pliable by warming them gently in a lightly greased non-stick frying pan.

Remove the tortillas from the pan and quickly spread with a layer of warm beans. Top each tortilla with grated cheese, onion, fresh coriander and a spoonful of salsa. Roll up tightly.

Just before serving, heat the non-stick frying pan over a medium heat, sprinkling lightly with a couple of drops of water. Add the tortilla rolls, cover the pan and heat through until the cheese melts. Allow to brown lightly, if wished.

Remove the tortilla rolls from the pan and slice each roll, on the diagonal, into about 4 bite-size pieces. Serve the quesadillas hot or cold, garnished with coriander leaves.

serves 4

4 ciabatta rolls

2 tbsp olive oil

1 garlic clove, crushed

for the filling

1 red pepper

1 green pepper

1 yellow pepper

4 radishes, sliced

1 bunch of watercress

115 g/4 oz cream cheese

ciabatta rolls

Slice the ciabatta rolls in half. Heat the olive oil and garlic in a saucepan. Brush the garlic and oil mixture over the cut surfaces of the rolls and set aside.

Halve and deseed the peppers and place, skin-side up, on a grill rack. Cook under a preheated hot grill for 8–10 minutes until just beginning to char. Remove the peppers from the grill and place in a polythene bag. When cool enough to handle, peel and slice thinly.

Arrange the radish slices on 1 half of each roll with a few watercress leaves. Spoon the cream cheese on top. Pile the roasted peppers on top of the cream cheese and top with the other half of the roll. Serve immediately.

serves 4

140 g/5 oz butter

1 onion, finely chopped

1 garlic clove, finely chopped

250 g/9 oz chicken livers

salt and pepper

1/2 tsp Dijon mustard

2 tbsp brandy (optional)

brown toast fingers, to serve

for the clarified butter

115 g/4 oz lightly salted butter

chicken liver pâté

Melt half the butter in a large frying pan over a medium heat and cook the onion for 3–4 minutes until soft and transparent. Add the garlic and continue to cook for a further 2 minutes.

Check the chicken livers and remove any discoloured parts using a pair of scissors. Add the livers to the frying pan and cook over quite a high heat for 5–6 minutes until they are brown in colour.

Season well with salt and pepper and add the mustard and brandy, if using.

Process the pâté in a blender or food processor until smooth. Add the remaining butter cut into small pieces and process again until creamy.

Press the pâté into a serving dish or 4 small ramekins, smooth over the surface and cover with clingfilm. If the pâté is to be kept for more than 2 days, you could cover the surface with a little clarified butter. In a clean saucepan, heat the butter until it melts, then continue heating for a few moments until it stops bubbling. Allow the sediment to settle and carefully pour the clarified butter over the pâté.

Chill in the refrigerator until ready to serve, accompanied by toast fingers.

serves 4

175 g/6 oz canned chickpeas

125 ml/4 fl oz tahini

2 garlic cloves

125 ml/4 fl oz lemon juice

salt

2–3 tbsp water

1 tbsp olive oil

1 tbsp chopped fresh parsley

pinch of cayenne pepper

for the crudités

selection of vegetables, including carrots, cauliflower and celery

hummus with crudités

Drain and rinse the chickpeas. Place them in a blender or food processor with the tahini, garlic and lemon juice and season to taste with salt. Process, gradually adding the water, until smooth and creamy.

Scrape the chickpea mixture into a serving bowl and make a hollow in the centre. Pour the olive oil into the hollow and sprinkle with the chopped fresh parsley and the cayenne.

Slice the raw vegetables into bite-sized portions and arrange on a large serving platter. Serve with the hummus.

serves 6

200 g/7 oz new potatoes

1 tbsp olive oil

1 onion, thinly sliced

1 red pepper, deseeded
and thinly sliced

2 tomatoes, peeled,
deseeded and chopped

6 large eggs

1 tbsp milk

2 tbsp finely grated
Parmesan cheese

sea salt and pepper

spanish omelette

Cook the potatoes in a saucepan of boiling water for 8–12 minutes until tender. Drain and leave to cool, then slice.

Heat the oil in an 18–20-cm/7–8-inch frying pan with a heatproof handle and cook the sliced onion and red pepper until soft. Add the tomatoes and cook for a further minute.

Add the potatoes to the pan and spread out evenly. Beat the eggs, milk and cheese, and salt and pepper to taste, in a bowl and pour over the potato mixture. Cook for 4–5 minutes until the eggs are set underneath.

Meanwhile, preheat the grill to high. Place the frying pan under the grill and cook the omelette for a further 3–4 minutes until the eggs are set.

Leave to cool, then cut into wedges and wrap in foil for a lunch box or spear onto cocktail sticks for a party snack.

serves 4

250 g/9 oz sushi rice

2 tbsp rice vinegar

1 tsp caster sugar

$1/2$ tsp salt

4 sheets nori

for the fillings

50 g/1$3/4$ oz smoked salmon

4-cm/1$1/2$-inch piece cucumber, peeled, deseeded and cut into matchsticks

40 g/1$1/2$ oz cooked peeled prawns

1 small avocado, stoned, peeled, thinly sliced and tossed in lemon juice

to serve

wasabi (Japanese horseradish sauce)

tamari (wheat-free soy sauce)

pink pickled ginger

mixed sushi rolls

Put the rice into a saucepan and cover with cold water. Bring to the boil, then reduce the heat, cover and simmer for 15–20 minutes, or until the rice is tender and the water has been absorbed. Drain if necessary and transfer to a bowl. Mix the vinegar, sugar and salt together, then, using a spatula, stir well into the rice. Cover with a damp cloth and leave to cool.

To make the rolls, lay a clean bamboo mat over a chopping board. Lay a sheet of nori, shiny-side down, on the mat. Spread a quarter of the rice mixture over the nori, using wet fingers to press it down evenly, leaving a 1-cm/$1/2$-inch margin at the top and bottom.

For smoked salmon and cucumber rolls, lay the salmon over the rice and arrange the cucumber in a line across the centre. For the prawn rolls, lay the prawns and avocado in a line across the centre.

Carefully hold the nearest edge of the mat, then, using the mat as a guide, roll up the nori tightly to make a neat tube of rice enclosing the filling. Seal the uncovered edge with a little water, then roll the sushi off the mat. Repeat to make 3 more rolls – you need 2 salmon and cucumber and 2 prawn and avocado in total.

Using a wet knife, cut each roll into 8 pieces and stand upright on a platter. Wipe and rinse the knife between cuts to prevent the rice from sticking. Serve the rolls with wasabi, tamari and pickled ginger.

makes 16

175 g/6 oz unsalted butter,
plus extra for greasing

3 tbsp clear honey

150 g/5¹/2 oz demerara sugar

100 g/3¹/2 oz smooth peanut
butter

225 g/8 oz porridge oats

50 g/1³/4 oz ready-to-eat
dried apricots, chopped

2 tbsp sunflower seeds

2 tbsp sesame seeds

sticky fruit flapjacks

Preheat the oven to 180°C/350°F/Gas Mark 4. Grease and line a
22-cm/8¹/2-inch square baking tin.

Melt the butter, honey and sugar in a saucepan over a low
heat. When the sugar has melted, add the peanut butter and
stir until all the ingredients are well combined. Add all the
remaining ingredients and mix well.

Press the mixture into the prepared tin and bake in the
preheated oven for 20 minutes.

Remove from the oven and leave to cool in the tin, then cut
into 16 squares.

makes 10

150 g/5$\frac{1}{2}$ oz white plain flour

100 g/3$\frac{1}{2}$ oz light brown self-raising flour

1 tbsp oat bran

2 tsp baking powder

$\frac{1}{2}$ tsp bicarbonate of soda

pinch of salt

50 g/1$\frac{3}{4}$ oz demerara sugar

1 tbsp clear honey

1 large egg

200 ml/7 fl oz buttermilk

150 g/5$\frac{1}{2}$ oz fresh blueberries

blueberry bran muffins

Preheat the oven to 180°C/350°F/Gas Mark 4. Line 10 holes of a muffin tin with muffin paper cases.

Mix the flours, bran, baking powder, bicarbonate of soda and salt together in a bowl and stir in the sugar. Whisk the honey, egg and buttermilk together in a jug.

Pour the wet ingredients into the dry and stir briefly to combine. Don't overmix – the mixture should still be a little lumpy. Fold in the blueberries.

Spoon the mixture into the paper cases and bake in the preheated oven for 20 minutes until risen and lightly browned.

Remove the muffins from the oven and leave to cool in the tin. Serve warm or cold.

makes 1 loaf

unsalted butter, for greasing

125 g/4$^1/_2$ oz white self-raising flour

100 g/3$^1/_2$ oz light brown self-raising flour

pinch of salt

$^1/_2$ tsp ground cinnamon

$^1/_2$ tsp ground nutmeg

150 g/5$^1/_2$ oz demerara sugar

2 large ripe bananas, peeled

175 ml/6 fl oz orange juice

2 eggs, beaten

4 tbsp rapeseed oil

honey, sliced banana and chopped walnuts, to serve

banana loaf

Preheat the oven to 180°C/350°F/Gas Mark 4. Lightly grease and line a 450-g/1-lb loaf tin.

Sift the flours, salt and the spices into a large bowl. Stir in the sugar.

In a separate bowl, mash the bananas with the orange juice, then stir in the eggs and oil. Pour into the dry ingredients and mix well.

Spoon into the prepared loaf tin and bake in the preheated oven for 1 hour, then test to see if it is cooked by inserting a skewer into the centre. If it comes out clean, the loaf is done. If not, bake for a further 10 minutes and test again.

Remove from the oven and leave to cool in the tin. Turn the loaf out, slice and serve with honey, sliced banana and chopped walnuts.